SCIENCE EXPLORER

JUNIOR

Think Like a Scientist in the Garden

by Matt Mullins

CHILDREN'S DEPARTMENT
Abington Free Library
1030 Old York Road
Abington, PA 19001

CHERRY LAKE PUBLISHING · ANN ARBOR, MICHIGAN

Published in the United States of America by Cherry Lake Publishing
Ann Arbor, Michigan
www.cherrylakepublishing.com

Content Editor: Robert Wolffe, EdD, Professor of Teacher Education,
Bradley University, Peoria, Illinois

Design and Illustration: The Design Lab

Photo Credits: Page 5, ©matka_Wariatka/Shutterstock, Inc.; page
8, ©Lisa F. Young/Shutterstock, Inc.; page 9, ©Eugene Moerman/
Shutterstock, Inc.; page 12, ©Guy Croft/Alamy; page 16, ©evan66/
Shutterstock, Inc.; page 18, ©REDAV/Shutterstock, Inc.; page 24, ©Trinity
Mirror/Mirrorpix/Alamy; page 28, ©Lucian Coman/Shutterstock, Inc.

Copyright ©2012 by Cherry Lake Publishing
All rights reserved. No part of this book may be reproduced or utilized in
any form or by any means without written permission from the publisher.

Library of Congress Cataloging-in-Publication Data
Mullins, Matt.
  Think like a scientist in the garden/by Matt Mullins.
      p. cm.–(Science explorer junior)
  Includes bibliographical references and index.
  ISBN-13: 978-1-61080-166-9 (lib. bdg.)
  ISBN-10: 1-61080-166-0 (lib. bdg.)
  1. Plants–Experiments–Juvenile literature. 2.
Science–Methodology–Juvenile literature. I. Title. II. Series.
  QK52.6.M85 2012
    580.72'4–dc22   2011006972

Cherry Lake Publishing would like to acknowledge the work
of The Partnership for 21st Century Skills. Please visit
www.21stcenturyskills.org for more information.

Printed in the United States of America
Corporate Graphics Inc.
July 2011
CLFA09

SEP 1 8 2014

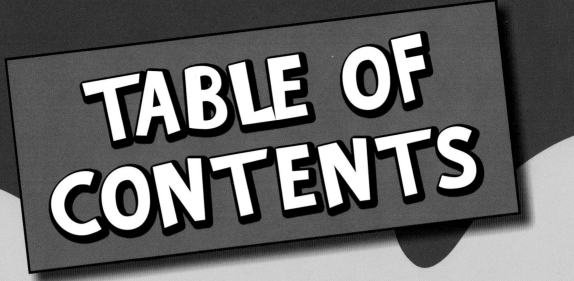

TABLE OF CONTENTS

How Does That Work? 4

Why Garden Outside? 10

Put a Patch on It! 16

How Acid Is Your Water? 22

Your Big Idea! 28

Glossary. 30

For More Information. 31

Index. 32

About the Author 32

How Does That Work?

Plants need water. Did you ever wonder why?

Have you ever looked at something and wondered, "How does that work?" Scientists do that all the time. Even in a garden.

Growing vegetables can help you learn a lot of science.

A garden is a fun place. Some people grow vegetables in gardens. Some grow fruits or flowers. You can learn a lot of science in a garden. What do plants need? What makes them green? What is their **environment** like? Scientists study **biology** and **chemistry** to find the answers to these questions. You can too—in your garden!

STEP-BY-STEP

You can get your own answers by thinking like a scientist. Go step by step. You may have to repeat some steps as you go.

1. Observe what is going on.
2. Ask a question.
3. Guess the answer. This is called a **hypothesis**.
4. Design an experiment to test your idea.
5. Gather materials to test your idea.
6. Write down what happens.
7. Make a conclusion.

Don't forget your notepad.

6

Use words and numbers to write down what you've learned. It's okay if an experiment doesn't work. Try changing something, and then do the experiment again.

Write down everything you notice during the experiment.

GET THE FACTS

A library is a great place to learn new things.

Scientists look for facts before they start an experiment. They use this information as a place to start.

Where can you find information? A library is filled with books, magazines, and science videos that can help you. Maybe there's a book on gardening at your house. You can talk to a teacher or a parent. You can visit a **botanical garden**, too.

You can also find facts on the Internet. Be careful. Not everything on the Internet is the truth. Ask an adult to help you find the best places to look for information.

Botanical gardens are filled with beautiful plants.

Why Garden Outside?

How do you keep plants healthy?

ASK A QUESTION

Plants are living things. They grow as big as they can when they have everything they need. They make seeds so they can make more plants.

Plants need water
and sunshine.

They usually grow best outdoors. What do you
think a plant needs so it can grow? Why are most
gardens outside?

A scientist named Gregor Mendel was very interested in peas. He grew 29,000 pea plants in a 7-year period. Mendel studied how to grow tall plants and short plants. He learned a lot about **traits**, such as being tall or short. He studied how traits get passed on by plants through their seeds to their **seedlings**.

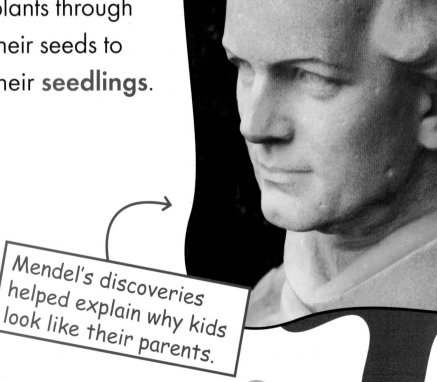

Mendel's discoveries helped explain why kids look like their parents.

Mendel studied the traits of peas.

Mendel's work with peas was important. He was a great scientist. He was also a terrific gardener! He grew his peas outside. Why do you think he chose to grow them outside? You can experiment to try to find an answer to that question.

DO AN EXPERIMENT

Plates will catch any water that drains from the bottom of the pots.

Start with four tomato plant seedlings. You can get these at a garden center. If the weather is warm, place two of them in a sunny spot outside. If it isn't warm, place two of them in front of a well-lit window. Place the other two in a dark cupboard or closet. Be sure to place small plates under all of them! Record in your notebook how tall each plant is. Write down how many leaves each plant has, too.

Water each seedling at the beginning of your experiment. Make sure the soil is damp. Check your plants every day for a week. Make sure the soil stays slightly damp. Water them as needed.

How do your tomato plants look at the end of the week? How tall is each plant? How many leaves does each plant have? Are all the plants still alive? Record what you observe about each plant. Which plants grew more? What can you conclude? You may want to keep observing your plants for a few more weeks to learn more.

The plants you kept in the cupboard might end up looking like this.

Put a Patch on It!

It is usually easy to spot an unhealthy plant.

ASK A QUESTION

Have you ever seen an unhealthy plant? Maybe the plant wasn't getting enough water. Maybe it was getting too much water. Maybe the soil was not nutritious enough. Sometimes other things can also hurt plants. We know plants need light, too. Our plants from the cupboard showed us that.

What color were the leaves of the unhealthy plants you saw? Do plants need sunlight to stay healthy even when they are full-grown? What do plants get from sunlight?

The color of a plant's leaves can tell you a lot about the plant.

Plants are complicated. Over the years, many scientists have discovered things about plants and how they grow. Chemists Pierre Joseph Pelletier and Joseph Bienaimé Caventou identified what makes plants green.

Pelletier and Caventou discovered why many plants are green.

Plants give off oxygen.

Jan Ingenhousz discovered that plants use light to create oxygen. Many scientists working together learned one important fact about plants. They use sunlight to create food.

Make sure you have everything you need.

What do you think will happen if you keep part of a plant out of the sun? Would it be healthy or unhealthy? Cut up some small pieces of brown paper. Then go into your garden with the paper. Bring along some paper clips.

Gently paper clip pieces of brown paper over some leaves on green plants. Leave the paper patches on the plants for a week. After 1 week, remove the paper. What happened to the leaves that were covered with paper? What can you conclude about sunlight and how plants stay healthy?

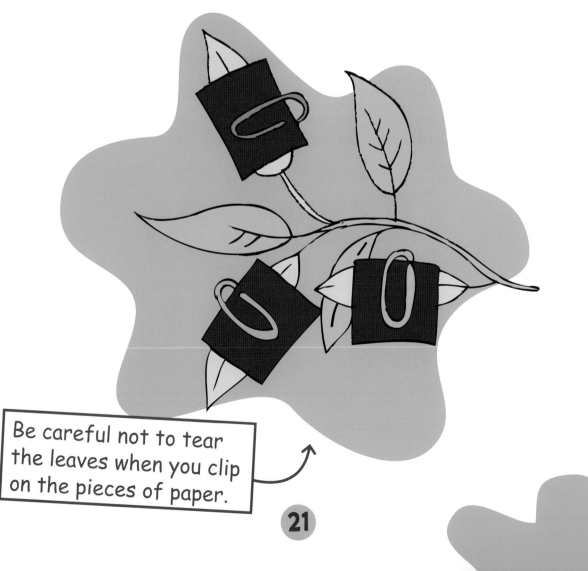

Be careful not to tear the leaves when you clip on the pieces of paper.

How Acid Is Your Water?

Air pollution is harmful to living things.

ASK A QUESTION

You have probably heard that some people are worried about air **pollution**. Air pollution is the junk that factories and cars put into the air. Gases come out of the big chimneys at factories and the pipes at the backs of cars. These gases stay in the air.

Then the gases mix with rain. In some areas, it creates **acid rain**. This can be damaging to farms. It falls on crops and hurts plants. It falls into lakes and streams and hurts fish. Insects can be hurt by it, too. Does acid rain fall on your garden?

Acid rain damages plants when they soak it up.

DO THE RESEARCH

Robert Angus Smith was a chemist who studied air pollution. He worked in Manchester, England, in the 1800s. Manchester had many factories. Its factories sent dark clouds of smoke into the sky. Smith studied the effect of this air pollution. He discovered acid rain in 1852.

Manchester's factories created a lot of pollution.

DO AN EXPERIMENT

You can find red cabbage at most grocery stores.

Do you think your garden gets acid rain? You can check your water for acid. Ask an adult to help you. You will need to wait for a rainy day. Set a small jar outside to catch rainwater. Inside, boil a head of red cabbage in a pot of water. Once the water has boiled, turn off the heat. Let the cabbage sit for 3 hours. Then strain the water into a container. Save the cabbage water.

Label each bowl so you don't get them mixed up.

Now cut a coffee filter into strips. Soak the strips in the cabbage water, and then lay them out to dry. After the strips are dry, set out three small bowls. Fill one with lemon juice. Fill another with water from your sink. Fill the third one with rainwater.

Dip one of your filter strips into a liquid. Hold it one-third of the way in for 5 seconds. Pull it out and watch the strip turn color. The darker red it turns, the more acid there is in the liquid. Compare each liquid. Which liquid has the most acid? Which one has the least? What can you conclude about acid rain in your area?

What do you notice about the filters?

Your Big Idea!

You probably have some questions about the plants in your garden.

You can study many plants in your garden. What different plants do you have? Do all the plants need exactly the same thing? Does it matter where in the garden they are planted?

You can come up with many ways to study plants and gardening. Maybe you want to see if you could add something to the soil to help the plants. What kinds of ideas do you have? What questions? Can you create an experiment for them? Of course you can—you know how to think like a scientist!

What will your next experiment be?

GLOSSARY

acid rain (AS-id RAYN) rain that picks up pollution from the air and becomes acidic

biology (bye-AH-luh-jee) the study of living things, including plants and animals

botanical garden (buh-TAN-i-kuhl GAHR-duhn) a garden for growing, studying, and showing people plants

chemistry (KEM-i-stree) the study of elements and their properties

conclusion (kuhn-KLOO-zhuhn) the answer or result of an experiment

environment (en-VYE-ruhn-muhnt) the place something is in

experiment (ik-SPER-uh-ment) a test of your idea

gases (GAS-ez) substances that fill whatever container you put them in

hypothesis (hye-PAH-thi-sis) a guess

pollution (puh-LOO-shuhn) dirty or damaging things that are added to the environment

seedlings (SEED-lingz) young plants grown from seeds

traits (TRAYTS) physical qualities of a thing, like height or weight

FOR MORE INFORMATION

BOOKS

Becker, Helaine. *Science on the Loose: Amazing Activities and Science Facts You'll Never Believe*. Toronto: Maple Tree Press, 2008.

Hoffman, Mary Ann. *Plant Experiments: What Affects Plant Growth?* New York: PowerKids Press, 2009.

WEB SITES

A Kid's Guide to Gregor Mendel—
The Father of Genetics
web.pdx.edu/~cruzan/Kid%27s%20Mendel%20Web/index.html
Visit this site to learn more about Mendel and his experiments with plants.

Plants for Kids
herbarium.desu.edu/pfk/index.html
Discover more information about plants and some activities you can do with them.

ABINGTON FREE LIBRARY
1030 OLD YORK ROAD
ABINGTON, PA 19001

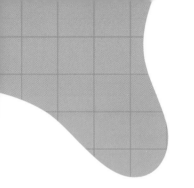

INDEX

acid rain, 23, 24, 25–27
air pollution, 22–23, 24

biology, 5

Caventou, Joseph Bienaimé, 18
chemistry, 5, 18, 24
color, 17, 18, 21
conclusions, 6

experiments, 6, 7, 8, 14–15, 20–21, 25–27
gases, 22–23

hypotheses, 6

Ingenhousz, Jan, 19
Internet, 9

libraries, 8–9

Mendel, Gregor, 12–13

notes, 6, 7, 14

observations, 6, 15, 17, 21, 27
oxygen, 19

Pelletier, Pierre Joseph, 18
plants, 10–11, 12–13, 14–15, 16–17, 18–19, 20–21, 23, 28–29

pollution, 22–23, 24

questions, 5, 6

research, 8–9, 12–13, 18–19, 24

scientists, 4, 5, 6, 8, 12, 13, 18–19
seedlings, 12, 14–15
seeds, 10
Smith, Robert Angus, 24
soil, 15, 16–17, 29
sunlight, 14–15, 17, 19, 20–21

traits, 12–13

water, 15, 16, 25–27

ABOUT THE AUTHOR

Matt Mullins holds a master's degree in the history of science. He lives in Madison, Wisconsin, with his son. Formerly a journalist, Matt writes about science, technology, and other topics, and writes and directs short films.